Raspberry Pi
Resource Guide

with some
Arduino on the side

Written By

Dr. Michael Stachiw

Edited by

Cathy Caligiuri

Raspberry Pi Resource Guide with some Arduino on the side

Table of Contents

Table of Figures

Introduction

Unlike most of the books on the market today about the Raspberry Pi (RSP), this book will not tell you that the RSP is the greatest thing to come along since sliced bread. We assume you already know that (or you wouldn't be reading this book), nor will we go through endless pages of what the difference is between each model of the RSP (see Appendix 1). This book is designed as a resource for all the things you want to do with the RSP, but didn't want to wade through hundreds of pages of reading books or web entries to find. With this said, this book will help you get an RSP up and running, connected to the internet, and outline several projects using your RSP. The majority of this book is filled with reference material, charts, graphs, diagrams, and other useful items we have found in our efforts at using the RSP.

The author's focus for the most part is how the RSP can be used in agricultural settings, but as we all know, agriculture is not just about farming. Today some of the most sophisticated uses of technology can be found on the farm, from automated milking parlors, to GPS driven tractors, to unmanned drones looking for insect damage to crops. As the saying goes, "it's not your grandfather's farm."

The current model of the Raspberry Pi is model 2B which has an on board Ethernet port, 4 USB ports, a HDMI video port, and an output jack for audio. It also has 40 pins in its General Purpose Input-Output (GPIO) connector. The original RSP only had 26 pins on its GPIO connector. Shown in Figure 1 is the basic layout of ports and connectors for a model 2 RSP.

Figure 1 - Raspberry Pi Model 2

The strength that the RSP provides to today's experimenter is that it is a complete multi-purpose computer that can be interfaced with the internet. This strength is also a shortcoming of the RSP. As we will see in some of the projects and throughout the sensor documentation, the RSP is basically a 3 volt system, whereas the sensor world is based on 5 volts. There is also the difference between the digital sensor and the analog sensors. To strengthen our toolbox for projects, we should also include reference to the Arduino computing device (see Appendix 2). The Arduino is not a full-multi use computer, instead it is a digital device that can sense and control objects in the physical world. Shown in Figure 2 is the layout of the Arduino Uno device.

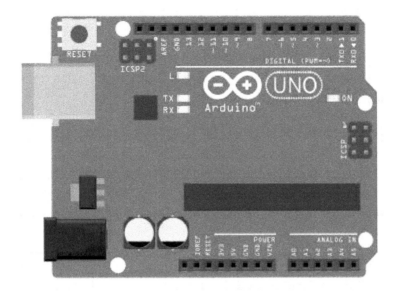

Figure 2 - Arduino Uno

The last item we will introduce is the breadboard (see Figure 3 and Appendix 3). The breadboard is a simple, clean way of putting together a group of components (diodes, resistors, switches, chips, etc.) and connecting them to the RSP or Arduino. Some smaller projects actually use the breadboard without the need for either the RSP or the Arduino.

What makes the breadboard crucial to electronic projects, is that components, wires, and the power source can all be connected together as desired without any soldering. And much like Legos or Lincoln Logs, can be changed around in a minute without any damage to the parts.

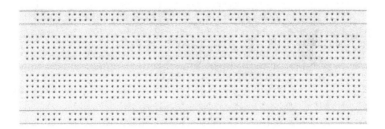

Figure 3 - Breadboard

Getting Started – Raspberry Pi

When your Raspberry Pi arrives, it will be in pieces and need to be assembled. For the most part, the assembly is easy and straightforward, but a couple of ground rules are needed before you start.

1) Never place the Raspberry Pi (RSP) on a metal surface if it is not in a case.
2) The power supply for the RSP and the monitor should be plugged into a voltage spike protecting power strip.
3) Never plug/unplug components from the RSP with the power plugged in.
4) The surface you place the RSP and its components needs to be dry.

To see descriptions and technical details on the various components required to get your Raspberry Pi running, see appendix 4. Figures 4 through 6 show the various places on the Raspberry Pi to plug in the required components. You need to make sure no power is attached to the board before you plug into the HDMI cable (or HDMI to VGA converter), micro-SD memory card, wireless networking dongle and wireless keyboard dongles. Now plug the power cord into your RSP. You are ready to run Raspberry Pi should look like the one shown in Figure 7.

USB Ports

Ethernet Jack

Figure 4 - Raspberry Pi

Micro USB for Power

HDMI Video

Audio port

GPIO Pins

Camera connector

Figure 5 - Raspberry Pi (continued)

Micro-SD
Card

Figure 6 - Raspberry Pi underside of card

Figure 7 - Raspberry Pi with cables & dongles plugged in

Now we're ready to plug in the power supply into the outlet and boot our Raspberry Pi.

One of the first things you will notice when you apply power to your Raspberry Pi, is the lack of sound. Unlike our Windows powered desktop and portable PC's, the Raspberry Pi makes no noise whatsoever. You have to be careful not to think it's not working and start unplugging cables and the like.

During the booting process, you need to keep your eye on the monitor/screen attached to your Raspberry Pi and the two LEDs (green and red) as shown in Figure 8.

Red power
Led and green
activity led

Figure 8- Power & activity LEDs

After a few minutes you should see the screen shown in Figure 9.

Figure 9 - NOOBS OS selection Screen

You need to select the version of Linux you wish to utilize on your Raspberry Pi. After you have selected the desired OS flavor, the system will start the OS setup. During this time, the screen will change and display various "promo screens" informing you about your selection of OS as shown in Figure 10.

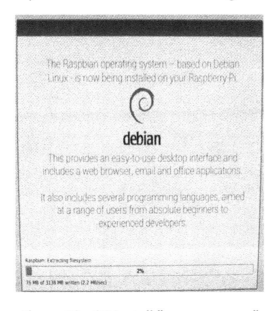

Figure 10 - OS Install "promo screen"

When the process has completed you will be presented with a confirmation screen as shown in Figure 11. You are now ready to reboot your Raspberry Pi into Linux.

Figure 11 - Completion of OS install

Accessing the Web

Even if you are not going to use your Raspberry Pi as an internet/network attached device, you need to set it up so it can access the network when needed. The biggest reason to setup your RSP for network access is for the downloading of new software required for these projects and updates to your core Raspberry Pi's operating Linux system.

The latest versions of the Raspberry Pi have an Ethernet jack and the device drives to use it. Wired access to your network and the internet is simply a matter of plugging one end of an Ethernet cable into your Raspberry Pi (see Figure 12) and the other end into your router.

Figure 12 - Ethernet cable plugged into Raspberry Pi

If your router, as most are, is configured for Dynamic Host Configuration Protocol (DHCP) then you are finished. If the router hasn't been configured for DHCP, get the router's management console connected to a PC and setup the DHCP.

If you are going to use wireless networking instead, you need to have a Linux/Raspberry Pi compatible wireless USB dongle. Depending on the version of Raspbain your Raspberry Pi is running, you can configure your wireless access two different ways. The older version supported a GUI interface utility that was accessible form the "preferences" menu, followed by the "Wi-Fi configuration" sub-menu option as shown in Figure 13.

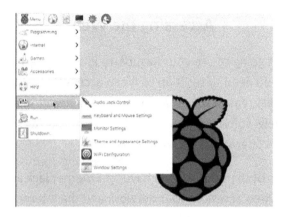

Figure 13 - GUI Wi-Fi Configuration Utility access

Selecting the "Wi-Fi Configuration" menu option will bring up the actual utility program as shown in Figure 14.

Figure 14 - Older Wi-Fi Configuration Utility

In the different tabs you can select the wireless network you wish to join and provide security key information as required.

The latest version of Raspbian uses a slightly different method to bring up the wireless configuration utility. You need to click on the "wireless" symbol located in the upper right hand of the graphical screen. This will bring up the utility program.

Supporting Projects

In this section, we will show you how to setup the Raspberry Pi as a standalone unit, file server, and as a web server. These projects are the building of useful tasks that can be supported by the Raspberry Pi.

Remote Access (Running Headless)

Running your Raspberry Pi (RSP) headless is a term meaning that you have set it up to be accessed and used without a locally attached monitor, keyboard, or mouse. The access to your RSP is done via the network, which we setup in the previous chapter. Before we start on this project, we have to make a decision: is the headless access going to be in text mode only (old style Unix) or a graphical desktop. In this section we will set it up both ways, and yes, you can have both methods available at the same time.

Text Mode Headless (SSH)

On your Raspberry desktop, click and start the LXterminal, and you screen should change to like that shown in Figure 15. To make sure the SSH server on your Raspberry Pi is running, at the $ prompt type:

sudo raspi-config

The screen should change to that shown in Figure 16.

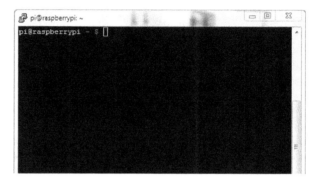

Figure 15 - Terminal Session

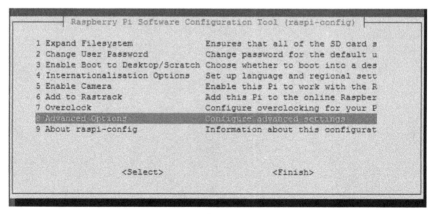

Figure 16 - Raspi-config program main screen

If your screen shows a menu option of "ssh Enable or disable ssh server" you can still precede you need to update your copy of the Debian distro Raspbian. To get to the SSH configuration option, move the selection bar down to "Advanced Options", and click. The screen will change to that shown in Figure 17.

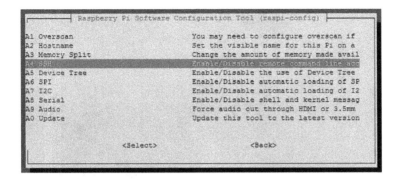

Figure 17 - Raspi-config advanced options

Move the selection bar to "A4 SSH," and click. The screen will change to that shown in Figure 18. Select "enable" from the options. You can now exit the raspi-config utility.

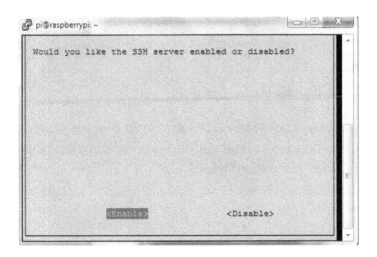

Figure 18 - SSH enable/disable screen

In order to access the Raspberry Pi computer from your desktop/portable computer using the ssh protocol, you will need to download and run the PuTTY[1] program and find out the IP address of your Raspberry Pi .

To find out the IP address, type the following:

ifconfig

---

[1] http://www.chiark.greenend.org.uk/~sgtatham/putty/download.html

You will be presented with a screen similar to the one shown in Figure 19. The information you are looking for is located in the "wlan0" block, and is indicated by: "inet addr: xxx where in this setup is 192.168.1.212

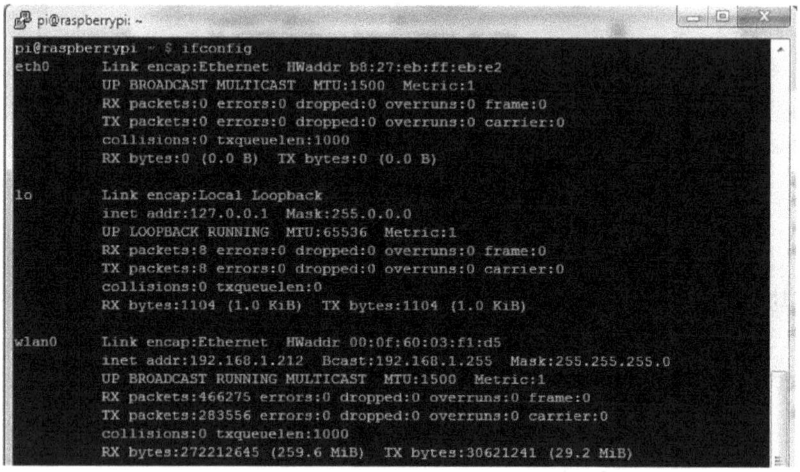

Figure 19 - Showing result of ifconfig command

Now you are ready to for the remote access.

After you have downloaded the PuTTY software for your desktop/portable computer, you simply run it. No installation required. You should be presented with a screen like that shown in Figure 20.

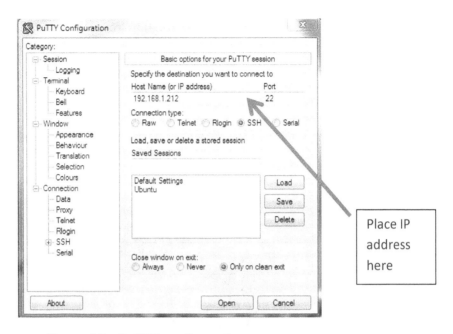

Figure 20 - PuTTY configuration screen

After entering your Raspberry Pi's IP address, click on the "Open" button. If all has been entered correctly, a terminal style window will appear on your PC's desktop with a login prompt. Your screen should look like the one shown in Figure 21.

Since the Raspberry Pi is running Linux, a multi user/multi-tasking operating system, you can expect a login request with password verification each and every time you remotely access the RSP computer.

Figure 21 - Typical Raspberry Pi login prompt

Unless you have changed the login information from the factory default, your login credentials should be:

User id: pi
Password: raspberry

A successful login should look like what is shown in Figure 22. It should be noted that you only get to enter the user id once.

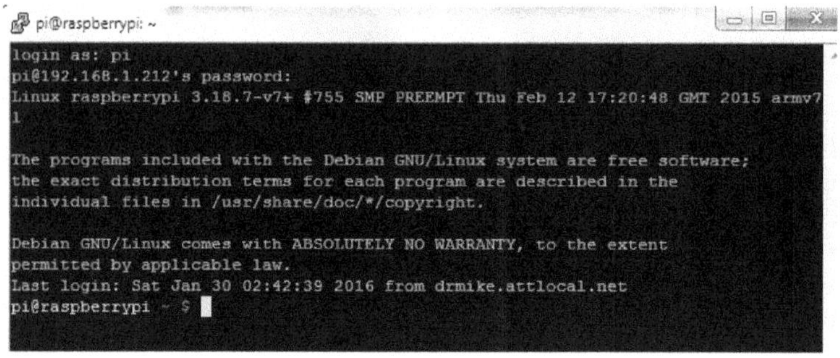

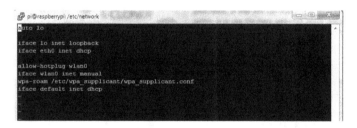

Figure 22 - Successful login to Raspberry Pi Computer

One problem with what we have done so far is that when we shut down the Raspberry Pi and restart it, our router will more than likely assign a new IP address. We will have to figure out this IP address by attaching a keyboard and monitor like we did earlier in this setup. The easy way to overcome this problem is to set the IP address so it remains constant. To do this will we edit the /etc/network/interfaces file with the vi editor[2]. Using the vi editor to open the file, we should see something like the what is shown in Figure 23.

Figure 23 - Original interfaces file

[2] Instructions on using the vi editor can be found in Appendix 11

We will replace the "iface eth0 inet dhcp" line with the following (shown in Figure 24):

Figure 24 - Altered interfaces file

The Dynamic Host Configuration Protocol (Dhcp) is useful for making network attachment of devices easier (you don't have to keep track of the devices IP address). In the case of a headless Raspberry Pi, it causes some problems.

Graphical Desktop Headless

If you want to access and utilize your Raspberry Pi remotely (headless) , and have the convenience of a graphical desktop, then setting up a TightVNCServer is the suggested path.

The first step is to download and install the TightVNCServer software on your Raspberry Pi computer. To download and install, type the following:

sudo apt-get install tightvncserver

After a couple of minutes the install should be finished. To start the server, type the following:

sudo tightvncserver :1

Please note that the ":1" indicates that port 5901 will be used in the connection protocol. You now need to install the TightVNCViewer software on your pc. The software can be obtained from: www.tightvnc.com

After installing the software, you need to run the TightVNCViewer software. After you start it, you will be presented with a screen similar to the one shown in Figure 25.

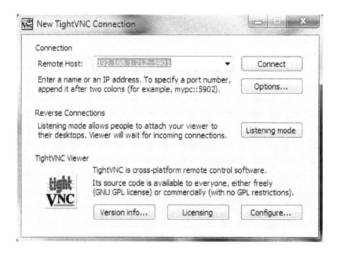

Figure 25 - TightVNCViewer Configuration

You will enter the IP address of the Raspberry Pi and ":5901" as the indicated port number, then click the "connect" button. After a few seconds a authentication screen like that shown in Figure 26 will appear. You will need to enter a password (it will ask for the password the first time, must be less than 8 characters, and will store that as the password) and then click the "ok" button. You will then be presented with the authentication screen shown in Figure 26, and a TightVNCViewer provided desktop shown in Figure 27.

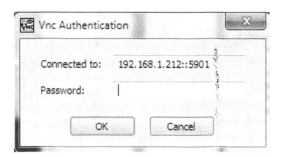

Figure 26 - TightVNC authentication screen

Figure 27- Graphical Desktop via TightVNCViewer

We have the same shortcoming as the text based headless setup. If the Raspberry Pi is shut down, when restarted the Dhcp will issue a new IP address, which we can only discover by connecting a monitor and keyboard to the RSP. To make the IP address be static, see the tail end of the text based headless setup section.

If we do reboot the Raspberry Pi, the TightVNC server will not be running. To start it, use your SSH headless connection and enter the following command:

Tightvncserver :1

This command, shown in Figure 28, will start the TightVNC server using port 5901.

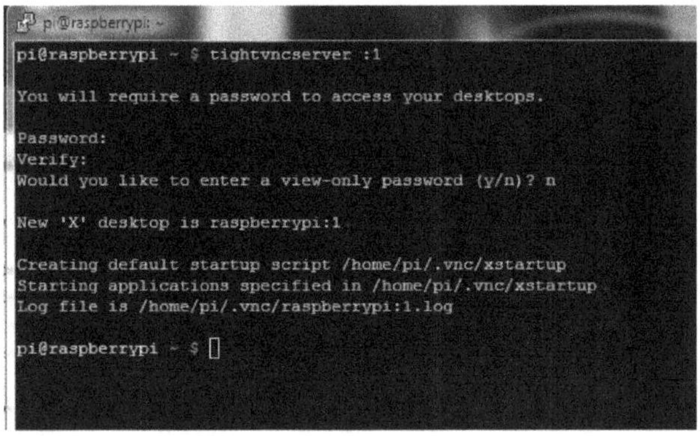

Figure 28 - TightVNCServer Startup

Network Attached File Storage (NAS)

Today, a networked environment is a must. Between sharing printers, file space, and the actual internet connection, a network is a necessity for today's modern work group. A common characteristic found in today's network is the concept of Network Attached File Storage (NAS). A NAS is where a simple server is used to host a file storage system, and in most cases enforce some security/sharing rules. Traditional NAS devices are expensive, and usually utilize proprietary hard drive hardware. This may sound like a less than ideal method of providing dedicated hard disk space, but when compared to a traditional file server, cost drives the equation. With our Raspberry Pi computer, we can drive the cost of NAS storage down even more, but we can also greatly reduce the overall energy requirements.

For this project, we will need our Raspberry Pi computer, but we also need one or two external hard drives with USB connectivity. Ideal external hard drives for this project would be the kind that are also powered by the USB connection, but we must keep in mind the limited amount of power provided by our Raspberry Pi's own power supply, so we will have to provide a powered USB port. If you wanted to provide only 8 or 16 GB of NAS served storage and were to utilize USB memory sticks, no external power would be required.

For this project, we used a 4 port powered USB hub and two 1 Terabyte (TB) external USB hard drives. The layout of hardware is shown in Figure 29.

Figure 29 - External Hard Drives & 4 Hub USB Port

From the perspective of the Raspberry Pi, we need to install the required software, which can be downloaded and installed by typing the following:

sudo apt-get install ntfs-3g

When the software has finished downloading and installing, you need find out if the system sees the external hard drives. To check, issue the following command:

sudo fdisk –l

this will result in a screen similar to that shown in Figure 30.

Figure 30 - Results of sudo fdisk -l command

The information shown in the first block (see Figure 31) is for the micro SD card that is running the Raspberry Pi.

```
        Device Boot      Start         End      Blocks   Id  System
/dev/mmcblk0p1            8192     1675781      833795    e  W95 FAT16 (LBA)
/dev/mmcblk0p2         1679360    15349759     6835200   85  Linux extended
/dev/mmcblk0p3        15349760    15415295       32768   83  Linux
/dev/mmcblk0p5         1687552     1810431       61440    c  W95 FAT32 (LBA)
/dev/mmcblk0p6         1818624    15349759     6765568   83  Linux
```

Figure 31 - Micro SD information

It is the second and third similar block of information provided by the fdisk command that we need for this project. The first 1TB drive is "sda1" and the second 1TB is"sdb1". Before we can mount these drives and make them available on the network, we need to create a directory to mount the drives against. For understandability, we will name these directories USBHDD1 and USBHDD2. You need to enter the following at the terminals command line:

sudo mkdir /media/USBHDD1
sudo mkdir /media/USBHDD2

We have created with the "mkdir" command two empty sub-directories off of the "/media" directory. We now need to mount the drives using the following commands:

sudo mount –t auto /dev/sda1 /media/USBHDD1
sudo mount –t auto /dev/sda1 /media/USBHDD1

Note: if these mount commands fail with a message like the one shown in Figure 32, then we will need to do a dismount of each, and then retry the mount command. To dismount, you would issue the following command for each:

sudo umount /dev/sda1
sudo umount /dev/sdb1

```
Mount is denied because the NTFS volume is already exclusively opened.
The volume may be already mounted, or another software may use it which
could be identified for example by the help of the 'fuser' command.
```

Figure 32 - Failure to mount message

With these drives mounted, we need to add a folder for the shared folders and files. To create these drives issue these commands at the terminal command line:

sudo mkdir /media/USBHDD1/shares
sudo mkdir /media/USBHDD2/shares

We now need to download and install the sharing software, which is named "Samba". To download and install the Samba software we use the command:

sudo apt-get install samba samba-common-bin

When the download and install is finished, the Samba needs to be configured. First, we need to make a backup copy of the Samba configuration file by issuing the following command:

sudo cp /etc/samba/smb.conf /etc/samba/smb.conf.old

Now we need to edit the Samba configuration file using the vi editor. To start the edit process, type the following:

sudo vi /etc/samba/smb.conf

In the Samba configuration file we need to change the following entries and add some additional information.

Find	Change To
workgroup =WORKGROUP	Change WORKGROUP to the name of your workgroup. For most users it is WORKGROUP so no change is required.
# wins support = no	wins support = yes
# security = user	Security = user

Find	Add
Go to the bottom of the configuration file.	[backup] comment = Backup Folder path = /media/USBHDD1/shares valid users = @users force group = users create mask = 0660 directory mask = 0771 read only = no

For our changes to the configuration file to take we need to restart the Samba server. To restart the server type in the following command:

sudo /etc/init.d/samba restart

Since we have turned on user level security, we need to create some accounts on our Raspberry Pi, which we will do by issuing the following command:

sudo useradd backups –m -g users
sudo passwd backups

The password will be asked for twice, you then need to add the "backups" as a user for Samba by typing the following command:

sudo smbpasswd –a backups

Restart the Samba server again by typing in the following command:

sudo /etc/init.d/samba restart

You will be prompted for "backups" password, which you need to enter.

To use the NAS shared drive, you would go to your Windows based PC and find the RASPBERYPI computer listed in your networks, and then provide the login credentials of:

User id: backups
Password: Password you provided when you set the account up

The last item we need to take care of is making sure that when the Raspberry Pi restarts, the external hard drives get mounted. We will use the vi editor. Type in the following command:

sudo vi /etc/fstab

and add the following two lines at the bottom of the file:

/dev/sda1 /media/USBHDD1 auto noatime 0 0
/dev/sdb1 /media/USBHDD2 auto noatime 0 0

Save the edited file and quit the vi editor.

Throughout this project, we have assumed that you have installed two external drives. Let's now proceed and setup a redundant backup between the first drive and the second. To install the required "rsync" software you need to enter the following command at the terminal prompt:

sudo apt-get install rsync

After the rsync software has been installed, you need to enter the synchronization command into the "crontab" utilities setup file. Type in the following command:

crontab –e

When the editor brings up the crontab scheduling file, we need to add the following line at the bottom of the file:

0 1 * * * rsync =av ==delete /media/USBHDD1/shares /media/USBHDD2/shares/

Save the changes to the file. We have finished our project of setting up a NAS file server with internal redundant backup capability.

Web Hosting[3]

One of the important building blocks you need to know is turning your Raspberry Pi into a web server. Now we must realistically realize that our Raspberry Pi will not power a full scaled website with thousands of visitors per day. Its hosting ability, however, cannot only support reporting the temperature and humidity of a Raspberry Pi driven weather station, it is also capable of running WordPress web hosting software for a limited number of users.

Setting up the Raspberry Pi as a webserver is pretty easy and straightforward. To start, get to a command terminal prompt and enter the following commands:

> **sudo aprt-get update**
> **sudo apt-get upgrade**

This will cause the Raspberry Pi to update and upgrade itself to the current operating system. To install the "Apache" web server software, we need to issue the following command:

> **sudo apt-get install apache2 php5 libapache2-mod-php5**

After the software has finished downloading and installing, we need to issue the following command to start the Apache server software:

> **sudo service apache2 restart**

To see the hosted webpage, you need to open a web browser (can be the one on your Windows PC or the one on your Raspberry Pi) and enter the following:

> **http://192.168.xx.yy**

---

[3] http://readwrite.com/2014/06/27/raspberry-pi-web-server-website-hosting

The actual web address is the IP address of your Raspberry Pi. If you don't know your RSP's IP address, then go to a terminal command prompt and type:

ifconfig

and you will find the IP address. If you wish to edit the default web page that is displayed, then you need to use vi and edit the page as indicated in the command below:

sudo vi index.html

There are some better tools for editing web pages than vi, and if you are looking to set up a multipage site (like an information library) then I would suggest installing the WordPress content management system on your Raspberry Pi.

Getting Started: Arduino Uno

Getting started with the Arduino Uno is much simpler than the Raspberry Pi. For initial use, all you will need to do is plug the USB cable into the Arduino and your PC, and download. Out of the box, your Arduino Uno should look like the unit shown in Figure 33.

Figure 33 - Arduino Uno

Before we go to hook your unit up to you PC, we need to cover a couple of ground rules are needed before you start.

1) Never place the Arduino on a metal surface if it is not in a case.
2) The power supply for PC should be plugged into a voltage spike protecting power strip.
3) Never plug/unplug components from the Arduino with the power plugged in.
4) The surface you place the Arduino its components, and your PC needs to be dry.
5) Never plug your Arduino into the USB at the same time you are using an external power supply. Use one or the other.

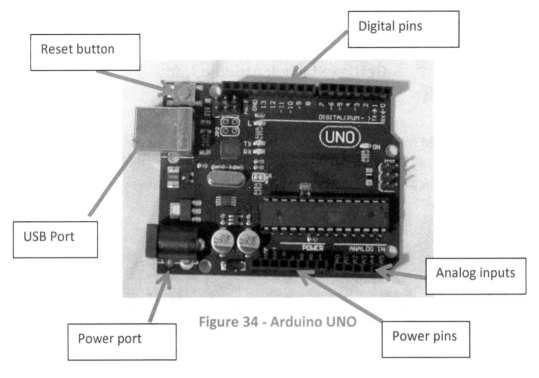

Reset button

Digital pins

USB Port

Analog inputs

Power port

Figure 34 - Arduino UNO

Power pins

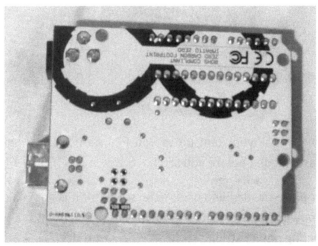

Figure 35 - Arduino UNO underside

We now need to install the Arduino device drivers and the Sketch programming support onto your PC. The required PC software can be downloaded from:

http://arduino.cc/en/Main/Software

Follow the instructions on the Web screen. After installation of the software, plug the USB cable into the Arduino and your PC. Figure 36 shows an Arduino plugged into a PC.

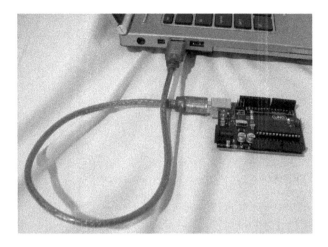

Figure 36 - Arduino Uno Plugged into a PC

To test that the Arduino and the software are all working together properly, you should enter the following Sketch program and run it.

```
//          Hello_World Program
void setup() {
  // put your setup code here, to run once:
  pinMode(13,OUTPUT);
}

void loop() {
  // put your main code here, to run repeatedly:
  digitalWrite(13,HIGH);
  delay(1000);
  digitalWrite(13,LOW);
  delay(1000);
}
```

Which should look like the screen as shown in Figure 37.

Figure 37- Sketch program to Blink Led

If you get an error about the Sketch software not being able to talk with the Arduino, you more than likely need to set the "com port" that the Arduino is located in on the PC. To set the port, in the Sketch software click on the "Tools" menu item, then the "Port" sub-menu item and select the port with "Arduino/Genuino Uno" listed.

If the Sketch program loads without any problem, you should start seeing the LED labeled "L" blinking on and off.

A couple of notes:

1) The blinking LED program will continue to run forever as written.
2) If you unplug the USB cable from the Arduino, and then plug it back in, the program will restart. This is very important! Unless you reset the

Arduino, the last program loaded will run when power is re-applied. To reset the Arduino, with no problematic programs running, you should load the sample program shown in Figure 38 into the Arduino.

3) Never plug your Arduino into the USB at the same time you are using an external power supply. Use one or the other.

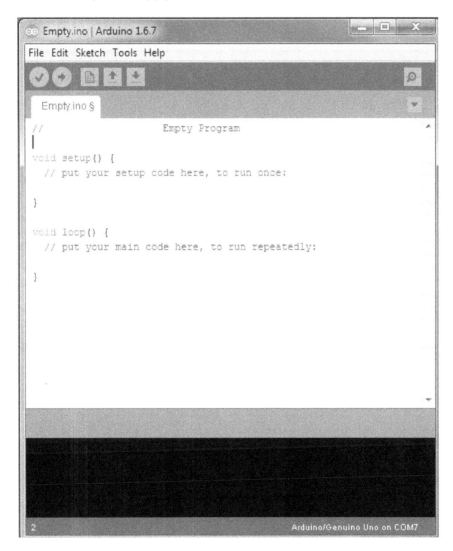

Figure 38 - Empty Program to reset Arduino

Basic Projects

The basic projects presented in this chapter are just that: basic projects. They were selected as a way to easily get the creative juices flowing on possible uses for the Raspberry Pi and the Arduino computing devices.

Before we delve into these projects, we need to review the very important rules to protect our Raspberry Pi and Arduino.

1) Never place the Raspberry Pi/Arduino on a metal surface if it is not in a case.
2) The power supply for the Raspberry Pi, and if a PC is used with the Arduino, should be plugged into a voltage spike protecting power strip.
3) Never plug/unplug components from the Raspberry Pi/Arduino with the power plugged in.
4) The surface you place the Raspberry Pi/Arduino, its components, and your PC needs to be dry.
5) Always triple check the wiring diagrams, photos, and assembly descriptions before applying power. It is very easy to fry your Raspberry Pi (and to some degree the Arduino) by hooking up the GPIO wires incorrectly and having voltage (especially the 5 volt sources required for most sensors) crossed with digital inputs.
6) Never plug your Arduino into the USB at the same time you are using an external power supply. Use one or the other.

Turning LED on/off[4]

One of the simplest projects in using your Raspberry Pi to control the outside world is to connect an LED and have the RSP turn it on and off. The Fritzing layout for this project is shown below in Figure 39.

---

[4] Raspberry Pi and breadboard images from Fritzing component library

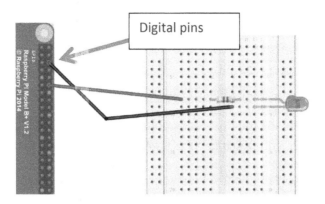

Figure 39 - Circuit to turn a led on and off

To create this circuit, you need an LED; two breadboard wires (male fitting on one end, female on the other), and a 470Ω resistor (yellow, brown, brown).

The actual circuit as implemented is shown in Figure 40.

Figure 40 - Blinking led project

To make the LED blink on and off, we will need to write a Python program. Start up the LXTerminal, and at the "$" prompt type in: sudo python3

Follow along with user input indicated in bold and followed by "<- you type in & hit the [enter] key":

> $ **sudo python3** <- you type in & hit the [enter] key
> Python 3.2.3 (default, Mar 1 2013, 9:15:23)
> Type "help", "copyright","credits" or "license" for more information.

>>> **import RPI.GPIO as GPIO** <- you type in & hit the [enter] key

>>>GPIO.setmode(GPIO.BCM) <- you type in & hit the [enter] key

>>>GPIO.setup(18,GPIO.OUT) <- you type in & hit the [enter] key

>>>GPIO.output(18,True) <- you type in & hit the [enter] key

The LED will turn on the minute you complete the last command into Python. To turn the LED off, you would need to type the following into Python:

GPIO.output(18,False) <- you type in & hit the [enter] key

Light Sensor

The next simplest project is having your Raspberry Pi measure something in the environment, in this case the level of light. The Fritzing layout for this project is shown below in Figure 41.

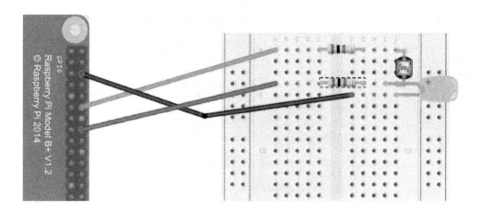

Figure 41 - Measuring light level project

Figure 42 - Measuring light level project as implemented

As the author of many Raspberry Pi & Arduino books, Simon Monk, indicates interfacing with the Raspberry Pi can be more difficult than the Arduino. The Python code to read the light level sensor is shown in Figure 43.

This code originated with Simon Monk, but has been modified to use standard input/ouput (STDIO). Using STDIO instead of the graphical interface the original program had, we can utilize a SSH terminal or TightVNCviewer to run the program.

```
# Light Meter
# Borrowed heavily from the code for the Electronics Starter Kit for the Raspberry Pi by MonkMakes.com
# changed from graphical interface for output, to stdio frienly output
# works via SSH and TightVNCserver
# February 3, 2016

import RPi.GPIO as GPIO
import time, math

# Configure the Pi to use the BCM (Broadcom) pin names, rather than the pin positions
GPIO.setmode(GPIO.BCM)

# Pin a charges the capacitor through a fixed 1k resistor and the thermistor in series
# pin b discharges the capacitor through a fixed 1k resistor
a_pin = 18
b_pin = 23

# empty the capacitor ready to start filling it up
def discharge():
    GPIO.setup(a_pin, GPIO.IN)
    GPIO.setup(b_pin, GPIO.OUT)
    GPIO.output(b_pin, False)
    time.sleep(0.1)

# return the time taken for the voltage on the capacitor to count as a digital input HIGH
# than means around 1.65V
def charge_time():
    GPIO.setup(b_pin, GPIO.IN)
    GPIO.setup(a_pin, GPIO.OUT)
    GPIO.output(a_pin, True)
    t1 = time.time()
    while not GPIO.input(b_pin):
        pass
    t2 = time.time()
    return (t2 - t1) * 1000000

# Take an analog reading as the time taken to charge after first discharging the capacitor
def analog_read():
    discharge()
    return charge_time()

# Take an analog reading as the time taken to charge after first discharging the capacitor
def analog_read():
    discharge()
    t = charge_time()
    discharge()
    return t

# Convert the time taken to charge the capacitor into a value of resistance
# To reduce errors, do it lots of times and take the average.
def read_resistance():
    n = 10
    total = 0;
    for i in range(0, n):
        total = total + analog_read()
    t = total / float(n)
    T = t * 0.632 * 3.3
    r = (T / C) - R1
    return r

# Getthe resistace information, and then
# using basic physics/eletronics equations
# convert to a temperature value
def read_temp_c():
    R = read_resistance()
    t0 = 273.15    # 0 deg C in K
    t25 = t0 + 25.0 # 25 deg C in K
    # Steinhart-Hart equation - Google it
    inv_T = 1/t25 + 1/B * math.log(R/R0)
    T = (1/inv_T - t0)
    return T

# Update the temperature reading and write to stdio
def update_reading():
    temp_c = read_temp_c()
    temp_f = temp_c * 9.0 / 5.0 + 32
    print('temp F=',temp_f)

# main loop of the program
# we use a simple do while loop to
# keep testing what the temperature is
while (1<100):
    update_reading()
print("Cleaning up")
GPIO.cleanup()
```

Figure 43 - Python Program to Read Light Levels

Temperature Sensor

A variation on the simplest project is to measure levels of light instead of measuring temperature. The Fritzing layout for this project is shown below in Figure 44.

The Python program to read the temperature sensor is shown in Figure 45.

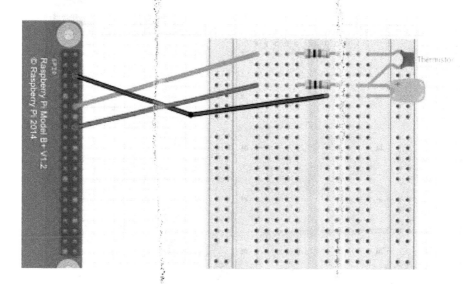

Figure 44 - Measuring Temperature Project

```
# Temperature Program
# Borrowed heavily from the code for the Electronics Starter Kit for the Raspberry Pi by MonkMakes.com
# chnaged from graphical interface for output, to stdio friendly output which
# works via SSH amd TightVNCserver
# February 3, 2016
#
import RPi.GPIO as GPIO
import time, math

C = 0.38    # uF
R1 = 1000   # Ohms
B = 3800.0  # The thermistor constant - change this for a different thermistor
R0 = 1000.0 # The resistance of the thermistor at 25C -change for different thermistor

GPIO.setmode(GPIO.BCM)

a_pin = 18
b_pin = 23

# empty the capacitor ready to start filling it up
def discharge():
    GPIO.setup(a_pin, GPIO.IN)
    GPIO.setup(b_pin, GPIO.OUT)
    GPIO.output(b_pin, False)
    time.sleep(0.1)

# return the time taken for the voltage on the capacitor to count as a digital input HIGH
# than means around 1.65V
def charge_time():
    GPIO.setup(b_pin, GPIO.IN)
    GPIO.setup(a_pin, GPIO.OUT)
    GPIO.output(a_pin, True)
    t1 = time.time()
    while not GPIO.input(b_pin):
        pass
    t2 = time.time()
    return (t2 - t1) * 1000000 # microseconds

# Take an analog reading as the time taken to charge after first discharging the capacitor
def analog_read():
    discharge()
    t = charge_time()
    discharge()
    return t

# Convert the time taken to charge the cpacitor into a value of resistance
# To reduce errors, do it lots of times and take the average.
def read_resistance():
def read_resistance():
    n = 10
    total = 0;
    for i in range(0, n):
        total = total + analog_read()
    t = total / float(n)
    T = t * 0.632 * 3.3
    r = (T / C) - R1
    return r

# Getthe resistace information, and then
# using basic physics/eletronics equations
# convert to a temperature value
def read_temp_c():
    R = read_resistance()
    t0 = 273.15      # 0 deg C in K
    t25 = t0 + 25.0 # 25 deg C in K
    # Steinhart-Hart equation - Google it
    inv_T = 1/t25 + 1/B * math.log(R/R0)
    T = (1/inv_T - t0)
    return T


# Update the temperature reading and write to stdio
def update_reading():
    temp_c = read_temp_c()
    temp_f = temp_c * 9.0 / 5.0 + 32
    print('temp F=',temp_f)

# main loop of th eprogram
# we use a simple do while loop to
# keep testing what the temerature is
while (1<100):
  update_reading()
print("Cleaning up")
GPIO.cleanup()
```

Figure 45 - Python Program to Read Temperature

The actual photo of this project is shown in Figure 46.

Figure 46- Measuring Temperature Breadboard

Detecting a Switch's Position[5]

One of the simplest sensors to setup and then detect is an on/off switch. In this project we utilize a Arduino and a simple on/off switch as shown if Figure 47.

Figure 47 -Arduino and Simple Switch

---

[5] Arduino and breadboard images from Fritzing component library

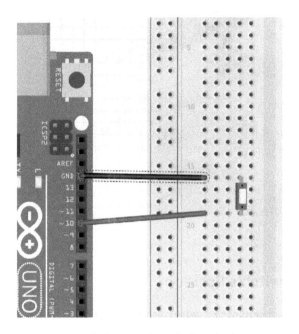

Figure 48 - Arduino and Switch Fritzing Layout

To detect if the switch is being pushed, the Arduino Sketch program shown in Figure 49 is loaded into the Arduino and run. When the switch is pressed the on-board LED labeled "L" will illuminate.

```
//                    Switch Program

int inputPin = 5;
int ledPin = 13;

void setup() {
  // put your setup code here, to run once:
  pinMode(ledPin, OUTPUT);
  pinMode(inputPin, INPUT);
  digitalWrite(inputPin, HIGH);
}

void loop() {
  // put your main code here, to run repeatedly:
  int switchOpen = digitalRead(inputPin);
  digitalWrite(ledPin, ! switchOpen);
}
```

Figure 49 - Sketch Program for Switch Project

The same project can be conducted using the Raspberry Pi. Shown in Figure 50 is a switch connected to the Raspberry Pi, and Figure 51 showing the Python code used to read if the switch has been pressed. The diplsay of the running Python is shown in Figure 52.

Figure 50 - Switch Detection Program Running

A variation for both the Arduino and Raspberry Pi would be to replace the switch with a tilt sensor.

```
# Switch
import RPi.GPIO as GPIO
import time
GPIO.setmode(GPIO.BCM)
GPIO.setup(3, GPIO.IN, pull_up_down = GPIO.PUD_DOWN)
while True:
 if(GPIO.input(3) ==0):
  print("Button pressed")
  time.sleep(1)
GPIO.cleanup()
```

Figure 51 - Switch Project for Raspberry Pi

```
pi@raspberrypi ~/mike $ sudo python gpio.py
gpio.py:8: RuntimeWarning: A physical pull up resistor is fitted on this channel!
  GPIO.setup(3, GPIO.IN, pull_up_down = GPIO.PUD_DOWN)
Button pressed
Button pressed
```

Figure 52 - Raspberry Pi Python Code for Switch Project

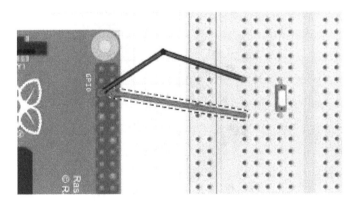

Figure 53 -Fritzing Diagram for Raspberry Pi Switch Project

Figures 54 and 55 show the tilt detector attached to the Raspberry Pi computer. Reading the tilt detector would use the same Python code as shown in Figure 51.

Figure 54 - Tilt Detector attached to Raspberry Pi

Figure 55 - Tilt Detector attached to Raspberry Pi, back view

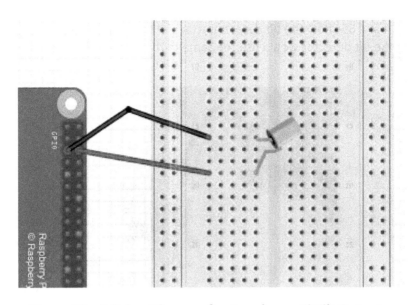

Figure 56 -Fritzing Diagram for Raspberry Pi Tilt Detector

Support Software

Fritzing

Fritzing is an open source (free) software tool for creating hardware designs. It runs on Windows 32 and 64 bit systems, Mac OS X, and Linux 32 and 64 bit systems.

The software allows you to document a Raspberry Pi and/or Arduino project in a clear, concise manner. It supports display of the project in three different views, with a source code view as well:

1) Breadboard view:

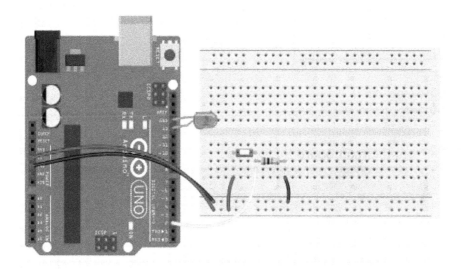

2) Schematic View:

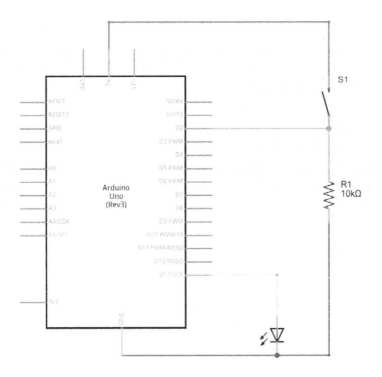

3) Printed Circuit Board (PCB) View:

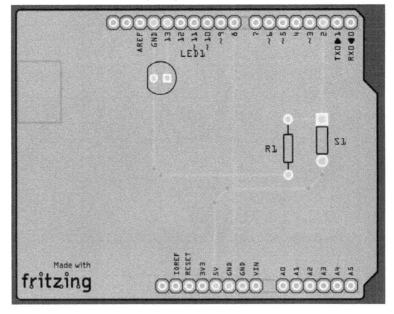

The printed circuit board view is especially useful if you plan on creating a circuit you will want to create custom printed circuit boards for. There is a service that can take your Fritzing circuit board diagram and produce the boards for you.

4) Source Code View:

```
/*
  Button

  Turns on and off a light emitting diode(LED) connected to digital
  pin 13, when pressing a pushbutton attached to pin 2.

  The circuit:
  * LED attached from pin 13 to ground
  * pushbutton attached to pin 2 from +5V
  * 10K resistor attached to pin 2 from ground

  * Note: on most Arduinos there is already an LED on the board
  attached to pin 13.

  created 2005
  by DojoDave <http://www.0j0.org>
  modified 30 Aug 2011
  by Tom Igoe

  This example code is in the public domain.

  http://www.arduino.cc/en/Tutorial/Button
*/

// constants won't change. They're used here to
// set pin numbers:
const int buttonPin = 2;     // the number of the pushbutton pin
const int ledPin = 13;       // the number of the LED pin

// variables will change:
int buttonState = 0;         // variable for reading the pushbutton status

void setup() {
  // initialize the LED pin as an output:
  pinMode(ledPin, OUTPUT);
  // initialize the pushbutton pin as an input:
  pinMode(buttonPin, INPUT);
}

void loop(){
  // read the state of the pushbutton value:
  buttonState = digitalRead(buttonPin);

  // check if the pushbutton is pressed.
  // if it is, the buttonState is HIGH:
  if (buttonState == HIGH) {
    // turn LED on:
    digitalWrite(ledPin, HIGH);
  }
  else {
    // turn LED off:
    digitalWrite(ledPin, LOW);
  }
}
```

The software is easy to use, very powerful, and is well thought out. A particularly powerful feature is that when you make a change in one of the views, all of the other views change to reflect the change as well.

To obtain a copy, go to http://fritzing.org

Python for Windows

If you are going to do a lot of programming using Python, you might want to obtain a copy for your Windows based PC. Two versions exist for Windows, a GUI version that acts much like IDLE Python (as shown in Figure57) and a command line version that acts much like Python when run from the LXTerminal (shown in Figure 58).

One issue you need to realize up front is that the Windows Python will not have access to the various Raspberry Pi specific libraries like RPI. GPO for example, as these libraries are hardware specific, and the GPIO pins used by the Raspberry Pi do not exist on your desktop/portable PC. However, for fine-tuning your general Python programming skills having access to the Windows version is a must.

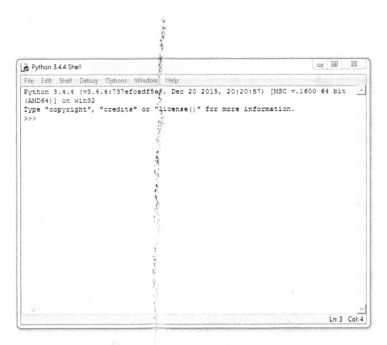

Figure 57 - Python GUI version

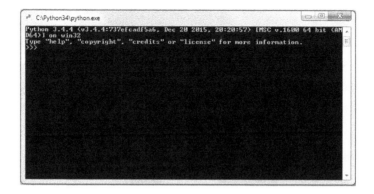

Figure 58 - Python command line version

To obtain a copy, go to https://www.python.org/downloads/qindows/

Arduino Sketch

If you are going to use an Arduino device as an interface with sensors and the Raspberry Pi, you will need to download a copy of the Arduino Sketch software from:

https://www.arduino.cc/en/Main/Software

and select the desired Sketch download. After download, run the installer and you should end up with a Sketch screen similar to that shown in Figure 59.

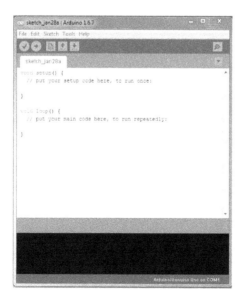

Figure 59 - Arduino Sketch Software

Appendix 1
Raspberry Pi

Raspberry Pi – Model A

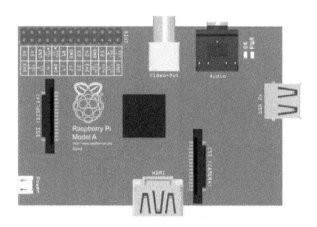

Technical Specification of Model A[6]

Technical Features

Chip	Broadcom BCM2835 SoC full HD multimedia applications processor
CPU	700 MHz Low Power ARM1176JZ-F Applications Processor
GPU	Dual Core VideoCore IV® Multimedia Co-Processor
Memory	256MB SDRAM
Ethernet	None
USB 2.0	Single USB Connector
Video Output	HDMI (rev 1.3 & 1.4) Composite RCA(PAL and NTSC)

---

[6] http://downloads.element14.com/raspberryPi1.html

Technical Features

Audio Output	3.5mm jack, HDMI
Onboard Storage	SD, MMC, SDIO card slot
Operating System	Linux
Dimensions	8.6cm x 5.4cm x 1.5cm

Raspberry Pi - Model B

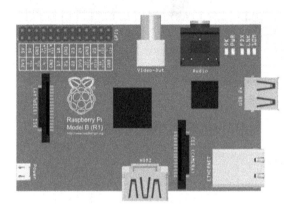

Technical Specification of Model B[7]

Technical Features

Chip	Broadcom BCM2835 SoC full HD multimedia applications processor
CPU	700 MHz Low Power ARM1176JZ-F Applications Processor
GPU	Dual Core VideoCore IV® Multimedia Co-Processor

[7] http://downloads.element14.com/raspberryPi1.html

Technical Features

Memory	512MB SDRAM
Ethernet	onboard 10/100 Ethernet RJ45 jack
USB 2.0	Dual USB Connector
Video Output	HDMI (rev 1.3 & 1.4) Composite RCA (PAL and NTSC)
Audio Output	3.5mm jack, HDMI
Onboard Storage	SD, MMC, SDIO card slot
Operating System	Linux
Dimensions	8.6cm x 5.4cm x 1.7cm

Raspberry Pi – Model 2

Technical Specification of Model 2[8]

- SoC: Broadcom BCM2836 (CPU, GPU, DSP, SDRAM)
- CPU: 900 MHz quad-core ARM Cortex A7 (ARMv7 instruction set)
- GPU: Broadcom VideoCore IV @ 250 MHz
- More GPU info: OpenGL ES 2.0 (24 GFLOPS); 1080p30 MPEG-2 and VC-1 decoder (with license); 1080p30 h.264/MPEG-4 AVC high-profile decoder and encoder
- Memory: 1 GB (shared with GPU)
- USB ports: 4
- Video input: 15-pin MIPI camera interface (CSI) connector
- Video outputs: HDMI, composite video (PAL and NTSC) via 3.5 mm jack
- Audio input: I²S
- Audio outputs: Analog via 3.5 mm jack; digital via HDMI and I²S
- Storage: MicroSD
- Network: 10/100Mbps Ethernet
- Peripherals: 17 GPIO plus specific functions, and HAT ID bus
- Power rating: 800 mA (4.0 W)
- Power source: 5 V via MicroUSB or GPIO header
- Size: 85.60mm × 56.5mm
- Weight: 45g (1.6 oz)

---

[8] http://arstechnica.com/information-technology/2015/02/raspberry-pi-2-arrives-with-quad-core-cpu-1gb-ram-same-35-price/

Raspberry Pi – Model B+

Technical Specifications of Model B+[9]

- Broadcom BCM2835 SoC
- 700 MHz ARM1176JZF-S core CPU
- Broadcom VideoCore IV GPU
- 512 MB RAM
- 4 x USB2.0 Ports with up to 1.2A output
- Expanded 40-pin GPIO Header
- Video/Audio Out via 4-pole 3.5mm connector, HDMI, or Raw LCD (DSI)
- Storage: microSD
- 10/100 Ethernet (RJ45)
- Low-Level Peripherals:
    - 27 x GPIO
    - UART
    - I2C bus
    - SPI bus with two chip selects
    - +3.3V
    - +5V
    - Ground
- Power Requirements: 5V @ 600 mA via MicroUSB or GPIO Header
- Supports Debian GNU/Linux, Fedora, Arch Linux, RISC OS and More!

---

[9] https://www.sparkfun.com/products/retired/12994

GPIO – Model A & B

3.3 V	●	●	5V
2 SDA	●	●	5V
3 SCL	●	●	GND
4	●	●	14 TXD
GND	●	●	15 RXD
17	●	●	18
27	●	●	GND
22	●	●	23
3.3 V	●	●	24
10 MOSI	●	●	GND
9 MOSI	●	●	25
11 SCKL	●	●	8
GND	●	●	7

Pin #1

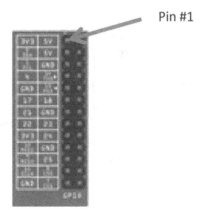

Figure 60 - Model A & B location of Pin #1 [10]

[10] http://wiringpi.com/wiringpi-and-the-raspberry-pi-compute-board/

GPIO – Model 2 & B+[11]

3.3 V	●	●	5V
2 SDA	●	●	5V
3 SCL	●	●	GND
4	●	●	14 TXD
GND	●	●	15 RXD
17	●	●	18
27	●	●	GND
22	●	●	23
3.3 V	●	●	24
10 MOSI	●	●	GND
9 MOSI	●	●	25
11 SCKL	●	●	8
GND	●	●	7
ID_SD	●	●	ID_SC
5	●	●	GND
6	●	●	12
13	●	●	GND
19	●	●	16
26	●	●	20
GND	●	●	21

Pin #1

Figure 61 - Model 2 & B+ location of Pin #1[12]

---

[11] http://openmicros.org/index.php/articles/94-ciseco-product-documentation/raspberry-pi/217-getting-started-with-raspberry-pi-gpio-and-python
[12] http://wiringpi.com/wiringpi-and-the-raspberry-pi-compute-board/

Appendix 2

Arduino

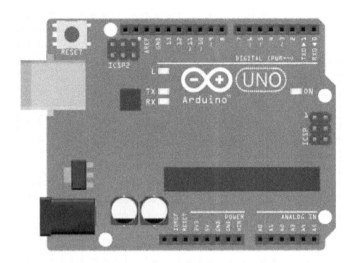

Technical Specifications

Microcontroller	ATmega328P
Operating Voltage	5V
Input Voltage (recommended)	7-12V
Input Voltage (limit)	6-20V
Digital I/O Pins	14 (of which 6 provide PWM output)
PWM Digital I/O Pins	6
Analog Input Pins	6
DC Current per I/O Pin	20 mA
DC Current for 3.3V Pin	50 mA
Flash Memory	32 KB (ATmega328P) of which 0.5 KB used by bootloader
SRAM	2 KB (ATmega328P)
EEPROM	1 KB (ATmega328P)
Clock Speed	16 MHz
Length	68.6 mm
Width	53.4 mm
Weight	25 g

Arduino Digital Pin	Port Pin
0	PD0
1	PD1
2	PD2
3	PD3
4	PD4
5	PD5
6	PD6
7	PD7
8	PB0
9	PB1
10	PB2
11	PB3
12	PB4
13	PB5

Appendix 3

Breadboard

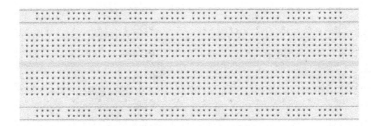

Figure 62 - Breadboard[13]

Please note that the real power/secret to breadboard (as shown in Figure 62) usage is understanding that the two outer columns (marked by red and blue stripes) are linked together, and that each row (in this image 5 holes) is linked together. To better see this relationship, see the Printed Circuit Board (PCB) view shown in Figure 63. A photo of an actual breadboard is shown in Figure 64.

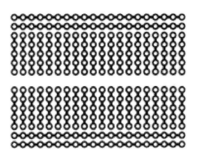

Figure 63 - Breadboard PCB View[14]

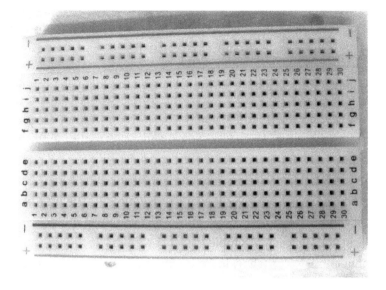

Figure 64 - Actual photo of a breadboard

Appendix 4
Key Components

In order to utilize your Raspberry Pi, you will need the following components.

1) Wireless keyboard with touch pad

You can use a regular USB keyboard and a USB mouse with your Raspberry Pi (RSP), but that means you will lose two USB ports for projects. Using a wireless keyboard with touch pad frees up a USB port, and it also makes it easier to work with your RSP. The other advantage of a wireless keyboard comes into play if you need multiple Raspberry Pi's in your project. A simple low-cost wireless keyboard and USB connection device (show in Figure 65 and 66) will work just fine. However, if you plan on using your RSP as a "work computer", a wired mouse and keyboard might be a better choice.

Figure 65 -Wireless keyboard & touch pad

Figure 66 - Wireless keyboard USB dongle

2) HDMI to VGA converter

Even though the developers of the Raspberry Pi (RSP) computer sing high praise for the latest version of the RSP having an HDMI port to connect to you TV or LSC display panel, most of us experimenting with the RSP use an old VGA monitor. An HDMI to VGA converter can be purchased at almost any retail electronics outlet. A typical converter is shown in Figure 67.

Figure 67 - HDMI to VGA converter

3) Wireless USB Dongle

If you are going to want to attach your Raspberry Pi to the internet, or a household network, you will either need to utilize the built in Ethernet plug (wired) or obtain a wireless USB dongle. Most of the USB wireless access dongle look much like the one shown in Figure 68. These USB wireless dongles are relatively cheap, but all of the Raspberry Pi books and web forums warn you to first check that the one you are buying will be compatible with the Raspberry Pi Linux distribution.

Figure 68 - USB Wireless Access Dongle

Appendix 5

Common Sensors

On the market today (eBay, Amazon.com, etc.) there is an abundance of low cost sensor kits advertised for the Raspberry Pi and Arduino devices. Unfortunately, there is little in the form of technical specifications and/or diagrams on their use. This section is provided as a starting point for the identification of these sensors, wat they look like, some indication of what they measure, and a starting point on their usage.

The sensors are generally divided into the following measurement areas:

- Biometric
- Humidity
- Infrared
- Sound
- Switches

Biometric

Item		Description
KY039: Heartbeat Sensor Module		This project uses bright infrared (IR) LED and a phototransistor to detect the pulse in the finger, a red LED flashes with each pulse.

Humidity

Item
KY015:

Temperature and
Humidity Sensor

Description
This DHT11
Temperature and
Humidity Sensor
features a calibrated
digital signal output
with the temperature
and humidity sensor
complex, ensuring the
high reliability and
excellent long-term
stability.

Infrared (IR)

Item
KY005:

Infrared
Transmitter Module

Description
Even though this is
not a sensor, it is
often used in
conjunction with the
IR receiver. This is
an infrared
transmitter module
that is used to emit
infrared signal.

KY022:

Infrared Receiver
Module

This is the infrared
receiver module,
with the following
features:
- Acceptance
  angle: 90 °
- Operating
  voltage: 7-5.5V
- Receiving
  distance:
  18Meter

Temperature

Item

KY001:

Temperature Sensor
Module

Description

This module
measures the
temperature and
reports it through
the 1-wire bus
digitally to the
Raspberry
Pi/Arduino.

KY013:

Analog Temperature
Sensor

This is an analog
temperature sensor
that outputs its
voltage in
proportion to the
temperature.

KY015:

Temperature and
Humidity Sensor

This DHT11
Temperature and
Humidity Sensor
features a calibrated
digital signal output
with the
temperature and
humidity sensor
complex, ensuring
high reliability and
excellent long-term
stability.

Item
KY028:

Digital Temperature
Sensor Module

Description
Digital temperature
module and a digital
interface.

Sound

Item
KY037:

High Sensitive
Microphone Module

Description
For sound
detection, module
has two outputs.

KY038:

Microphone Module

Microphone sound
sensor for Arduino.

Switches (open/closed)

Item		Description
KY003: Hall Magnetic Field Sensor Module		This module can be used to detect the presence of magnetic field. This can be used for a magnetic switch (i.e. door open or closed).
KY004: Momentary Button Module		This is a button switch module.
KY017: Quicksilver Switch Module - Tilt Switch		A tilt switch that can turn on and off depending on the tilt position. The switch is mercury.

Item		Description
KY020: Tilt Switch Module		Tilt switch module and a digital interface.
KY021: Mini Reed Switch Module	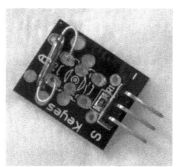	Reed switch.
KY024: Linear Magnetic Hall sensor		Linear Hall magnetic module and a digital interface.
KY027: Magic LED Cup Module		This module has two parts - an LED and a mercury tilt switch.

Appendix 6
Linux Shell Commands

Linux commands are all lowercase. This is by no means a complete list of Linux shell commands, simply the most used.

Command	Description
cat [filename]	Lists the contents of a file to the terminal screen
cd	Change directory
chmod [filename]	Changes the permissions on a file
chown [filename]	Changes who owns a file
clear	Clears the terminal screen
date	Used to display and/or change the operating system date
df	Disk Free, display how much free disk space remains
kill	Kill or stop a process
lpr	Send a file to the printer
ls	List files in current directory
mkdir	Make or create a directory
mv	Move a file from one directory to another
ps	Show what processes are currently running
pwd	Print Working Directory. Informs you what directory you currently are working in.
rm	Remove. Delete or remove a file
rmdir	Remove or delete a directory

Command	Description
su	Substitute User. Allows issuing a command at a different user level.
who	Show what users are logged onto the system
whoami	Who Am I. Which user is logged into the system

Appendix 7
Linux Directory Structure

```
/ <-- -- -- root directory
|--/bin
|--/boot
|--/dev
|--/etc
|--/home
|--/lib
|--/mnt
|--/opt
|--/sbin
|--/tmp
|--/usr
|--/var
|--/root
```

Directory	Description
/bin	Essential user command binaries used for general operations: The Linux shell command binary (program) files are located here.
/boot	Static files of the boot loader. Files here are necessary for a Linux system to start.
/dev	Where the device (driver) files are located.
/etc	Configuration files for all programs. Usually text files with options specified.
/home	Home directories for all the users to store personal files.

Directory	Description
/lib	Essential shared libraries and kernel modules.
/media	Mount point for removable media.
/mnt	Temporary mounted file systems.
/opt	Add on application software packages.
/sbin	Essential system binaries.
/tmp	Programs write their temporary files here.
/usr	Multi-user utilities & applications.
/var	Variable data on a system. Log files & backups are located here.
/root	Home directory for root.
/proc	Virtual directory containing process information.

Appendix 8
Python Reference

When starting the Windows version of Python, you have two options:

1) Star the Python (command line)
2) Start the Python GUI

Command Line:

When starting Python (command line), you have options that can be specified on the command line.

python [option] ... [-c cmd | -m mod | file | -] [arg] ...

-c cmd : program passed in as string (terminates option list)

-d   : debug output from parser (also PYTHONDEBUG=x)

-E   : ignore environment variables (such as PYTHONPATH)

-h   : print this help message and exit

Python GUI

One of the nice features of the Windows GUI version of Python, is that at the top of most menus, there is a dotted line referred to as the "tear it off", which allows you to have that menu be detached from the main GUI screen. This is very helpful if you are using help and doing programming.

Reserved Words: These are words that cannot be used as variable names. They have special meaning and functionality within the python environment

and	exec	not
assert	finally	or
class	from	print
continue	global	raise
def	if	return
del	import	try
elif	in	while
else	is	with
except	lamba	yield

Variables:

Variables in Python cannot start with a number or have embedded spaces. The following indicate legal/illegal variables names:

a cow	Illegal, embedded space
a_cow	Legal
1cow	Illegal, starts with a number
A_pig	Legal, but considered bad style because of the starting capital. Better would be a_Pig

Some Key Notes:

1) Strings are immutable. Once a string has been created, it cannot be changed.
2) All programming "commands" or "elements" are in lower case. For example, it is "print" not "Print".
3)

Command:			
#	**Details:**		Comment. Any text after the # is ignored by the Python language.
	Example:		# this is a comment line print("hello") # this prints hello
\	**Details:**		Line joining. Used if a line of code is going to span several lines in the file. A comment (#) cannot follow the \. Nothing can follow the \ if it's being used to continue on a second line.
	Example:		If piglegs< 4 \ And cowlegs=4: Return 1
	Example:		The \ when used within a string "escapes" the next character. For example: "mike\'s pig"

Command:		
		The \ prevents the ' from being interpreted as a single quote used to terminate a string.
	Example:	The \ when used in a string can also be used to indicate an escape sequence. For example: "mike\n123 memory ln" Would cause the output to look like: Mike 123 memory ln Where the \n inserts the escape character for new line
=	**Details:**	Used to assign a value. Target variable is on the left side of the "=", while variables/values which will be used in the assignment go on the right hand side of the "=".
	Example:	X=5 + 5
for	**Details:**	For is the start of a looping statement. for_stmt ::= "for" target_list "in" expression_list ":" suite ["else" ":" suite] The "for" statement is used to iterate over the elements of a sequence (such as a string, tuple or list) or other iterable object.
	Example:	for j in range(5): print(j)
print	**Details:**	print(value, ..., sep=' ', end='\n', file=sys.stdout, flush=False) Optional keyword arguments: file: a file-like object (stream); defaults to the current sys.stdout. sep: string inserted between values, default a space. end: string appended after the last value, default a newline. flush: whether to forcibly flush the stream. By default, a "newline" character is added to the end of each print() statement. To prevent advancing to a

Command:		
		new line, use the "end=" in the print statement. For example: print('pig', end='')
	Example:	print("Hello world")
format()	Details:	Format is useful when printing to replace "bookmarks" with the value of a variable(s).
	Example:	cowsfeet=4 chickenwings=2 breed="duroc' print('a cow has {0} feet'.format(cowsfeet)) print('{0} is mikes favorite breed of pig',format(breed)) would result as: a cow has 4 feet Duroc is Mikes favorite breed of pig
exit()	Details:	Used to quit the Python interpreter
	Example:	Exit()

Arithmetic Operators:

Programming Element:	Description:
=	Element on left side of "=" is assigned the value expressed on the right hand side of the "=".
+	Two numeric values or variables are added together. Can be numbers or strings.
-	Numeric value or variable on left hand side of "-" has the numeric or variable on the right hand side of the "-" subtracted.
*	Two numeric values of variable are multiplied together.
/	Numeric value or variable on left hand side of the "/" is divided by the numeric value or variable on the right hand side of the "/".
%	Calculated the remainder when numeric value or variable on right hand side of the "%" is divided by the numeric value or variable on the right hand side of the "%".

Escape Sequences:

Escape Sequence:	Description:
\a	Ring the bell.
\f	Form feed.
\n	New line.
\r	Carriage return.
\t	Tab, horizontal.
\v	Tab, vertical.
\xhh	Asci character with the hex value of hh.

Modules:

Module:	Description
string	Supports common string operations.
math	Supports math operations and constants.
cmath	Support for complex math.
re	Support for regular expressions.
fileinput	Support for text files.

Comparison Operators:

Programming Element:	Description:
==	Equal to.
!=	Not equal.
<	Less than.
>	Greater than.
<=	Less than or equal to.
>=	Greater than or equal to.
<>	Not equal to.

Appendix 9
Arduino Software

Before you can use the Arduino hardware, you will need to download and install the required drivers and Sketch software from the Arduino website.

Go to: http://arduino.cc/Main/Software

After installing the downloaded software, you will be presented with the Sketch programming environment, which should look like Figure 69.

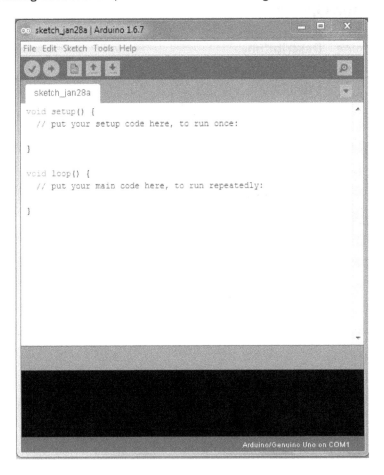

Figure 69 - Sketch programming environment

Appendix 10
Sketch Reference

Sketch is the programming language utilized by the Arduino family of products. The program is usually created on a PC running Windows, Linux, or Mac, and loaded onto the Arduino device. It can also be loaded via the Raspberry Pi computer. Sketch can be divided into four parts: syntax, structure, values, and functions. The online reference for sketch can be found at:

https://www.arduino.cc/en/Reference/HomePage

Some key items

1) Capitalization of structure elements, variables and functions is for the most part lower case
2) #1 is not true for multiword functions and some constants
3) If the compiler comes back with a "xxx not" found error, check the manual for capitalization first.
4) Indentation of the code does not matter to the compiler, but good indentation does help with code maintenance.

Syntax:

Programming Element:	Description:
;	Semicolon. Used to end a statement. Used much the same as in Delphi/Pascal. Required at the end of each functional line. For example: X = Y / 12;

{}	Curly braces. Always used as a pair, or balanced. Much like the "Begin" and "end" key words in Delphi/Pascal. Use in this language is similar to use in the "C" programing language, marks the beginning and end of a block of code. For example:
	    Void Setup() {
	    pinMode(13,OUTPUT);
	    }

//	Double forward slashes. Used to indicate a single line comment. May be on a line by itself, or training a functional line. Not functional code.

Programming Element:	Description:

	For example:
	
	    // Set pin 13 for output
	    pinMode(13.OUTOUT); // output

/* */	Forward Slash star & star forward slash. Always used as a pair or balanced. Similar to the (* and *) used in Delphi/Pascal. Indicates a multi-line comment. Not functional code. For example:
	
	    /*
	    Bug patch
	    1/6/1958
	    Dr. Stachiw
	    */

#define	Used to define a constant used throughout the program. Can cause bugs and is not recommended. The "=" and ";" are not used in this statement. Use example: #define pi 3.143456
#include	Used to "include" a library (external program code). The "=" and ";" are not used in this statement. Use example: #include <stdio.h>

Structure:

The simplest Sketch program is:

```
void setup() {
}
void loop() {
}
```

The "setup" and "loop" sections represent the outermost or highest level of structure in a Sketch program.

Programming Element:	Description:
setup()	The "setup" section of the program is loaded & run first and only once. Defining variables, pin modes, and which libraries to include are usually done in this section of the program.
loop()	The "loop" section is a looping section, but it needs to be realized that this is an endless loop. Reading of sensors, for example, takes place in this section.

Control Structures:

Programming Element:	Description:

If ()	Comparison and conditional. Used to evaluate an expression. For example:
	
	    If (X<3.14245)
	    {
	      digitalWrite(13, HIGH);
	    }
	
	Note that the expression being evaluated is in ()'s and the use of the {}'s to mark the beginning and end of the block of code controlled by the "if" statement. If the result of "if" is a single line statement, the {}'s are optional, but coding is more clear if left in.

If () else	Comparison with multiple outcomes. Used to evaluate an expression, with true and false going to separate blocks of code. For example:
	
	    If (X<3.14245)
	    {
	    digitalWrite(13, HIGH);
	    }
	    else
	    {
	    digitalWrite(13,LOW);
	    }
	The "else" can lead to another "if" test if needed.

for ()	More appropriately referred to as the "for loop", which causes the code to loop through a set of code. The syntax of this element is basically the same as that found in the "C" programming language. The code within the ()'s is the instructions on how long the loop is to run.
	
	For example:
	    for (int J=1; J <20; J++)
	    {
	    Println(j);
	    }

Programming Element:	Description:
	Where the looping variable "J" is defined to have an initial value of 1, will increase by 1 (J++) through to 19 (J<20).

switch() case	The "switch case" is a multi-conditional statement. For example:
	
	``
	switch(j){
	case 10:
	   println(j);
	   break;
	case 20:
	   println(j/20);
	   break;
	}
	``
	
	Where is the variable j=10 then the first block of code between the "case 10;" and "break;" is executed, if j=20, then the second block of code gets executed. Also support for a "default:" situation.

while()	A "while" loop will run indefinitely, until the specified condition is met. For example:
	
	``
	x=5
	while (x<25)
	{
	digitalWrite(13,HIGH);
	 delay(1000);
	digitalWrite(13,HIGH);
	 delay(1000);
	x++;
	}
	``
	
	Where X is initially set to a value of 5, and while X is less than 25, we will loop and turn the LED on/off. At the bottom of the block of code we add 1 to the value of x.

do .. while	"Do while" loops work similar to the while loop, but the big difference is that the tested condition is at the bottom.

Programming Element:	Description:

	For example:
	
	    x=5
	    do
	    {
	    digitalWrite(13,HIGH);
	     delay(1000);
	    digitalWrite(13,HIGH);
	     delay(1000);
	    x++;
	    }
	    while (x<25)

break	Used to break (break out) from a do, for, or while loop as well as the "switch case". For example:
	
	    for (int J=1; J <20; J++)
	    {
	    println(j);
	    if (temp>212)
	    {
	    break;
	    }
	    }
	
	This code will loop from 1 to 19, unless the temperature rises above 212.

return	Used to terminate a function and indicate the "return" value from the function. For example:
	int inchestofeet()
	{
	return inches/12;
	}

goto	Forces a jump in the execution of the code to a specific point. Jump point is defined by "label:" and the related "goto" would be "label;"

Arithmetic Operators:

Programming Element:	Description:
=	Element on left side of "=" is assigned the value expressed on the right hand side of the "=".
+	Two numeric values or variables are added together.
-	Numeric value or variable on left hand side of the "-" has the numeric or variable on the right hand side of the "-" subtracted.
*	Two numeric values of variable are multiplied together.
/	Numeric value or variable on left hand side of the "/" is divided by the numeric value or variable on the right hand side of the "/".
%	Calculated the remainder when numeric value or variable on right hand side of the "%" is divided by the numeric value or variable on the right hand side of the "%".

Comparison Operators:

Programming Element:	Description:
==	Equal to.
!=	Not equal.
<	Less than.
>	Greater than.
<=	Less than or equal to.
>=	Greater than or equal to.

Variables:

Variables and their related programing structures are the key elements that make a computer program really useful. By definition, a variable is an element that takes on a value, but that value can be changed throughout the program. In contrast, a constant maintains a fixed value throughout a program's life.

Programming Element:	Description:
false	Is given an internal value of 0.
true	Is given an internal value of 1.
HIGH	If used in the reading of a pin, means that the voltage reached required level. If used in the writing of a pin, pins voltage is set to correct level.
LOW	If used in the reading of a pin, voltage has not reached required level. If used in the writing of a pin, voltage is set to 0.

Data Types:

Programming Element:	Description:

void	Used in function declarations to indicate there will be no return value from the function. For example:
	    void setup()
	    {
	    }

boolean	Variable hold value of true or false.
char	Variable hold only a single character, which during assignment is enclosed in single quotes ('z').
unsigned char	A variable with value between 0 and 255. Byte is preferred data type.
byte	A variable with value between 0 and 255.
int	A variable with values in the range of -32,000 to 32,000.
unsigned int	A variable with values in the range of 0 to 65,000.
long	A variable with a very large integer range, both positive and negative. Long number when assigned has to be followed by an "L".
short	A variable that has a storage range the same as an int.
float	A variable where the numeric value has a decimal point. Very large and both negative and positive. Only accurate to 7 decimal places.
double	Same as float.
String	Variable with alphabetic charters. Notice that "string" starts with a capital "S".

Programming Element:	Description:
array	Variable with an array of values. When declared, type goes first then variable. For example: int pig[]; int cow[4] ={1,2,3,4};

Functions:

Programming Element:	Description:
pinMode()	Configures specified pin as input or output. Syntax is: pinMode(pin,mode); with mode being: INPUT, OUTPUT, or INPUT_PULLUP
digitalRead()	Reads the value from the specified pin. Syntax is: digitalRead(pin); Value is either HIGH or LOW
digitalWrite()	Write a HIGH or LOW value to specified pin. Syntax is: digitalWrite(pin);
analogReference()	Configures reference voltage.
analogRead()	Reads the value from the specified pin. Syntax is: analogRead(pin);
analogWrite()	Writes an analog wave value to the specified pin. Syntax is: analogWrite(pin);
tone()	Generates square wave, which can be used with a buzzer to generate a specified tone. Syntax is: tone(pin,frequency);

Programming Element:	Description:
noTone()	Stops the generation of the square when on the indicated pin. Syntax is: noTone(pin);
millis()	Number of milliseconds before the Arduino board begins running the program.
micros()	Number of microseconds before the Arduino board begins running the program
delay()	Causes a pause in the program's execution for the specified milliseconds.
delayMicroseconds()	Causes a pause in the programs execution for the specified microseconds.
max()	Calculates the maximum of two numbers. Syntax is: max(num1,num2);
min()	Calculates the minimum of two numbers. Syntax is: max(num1,num2);
abs()	Calculates the absolute value of a number. Syntax is: abs(num);
constrain()	Calculates if a number falls within a range, returns the number if it is. But if higher or lower than the range, it returns the boundary number. Syntax is: Constrain(num1,lower boundry, upper boundary);
sqrt()	Calculates the square root of a number. Syntax is: Sqrt(num);
isAlphaNumeric()	Validates if the character passed is alphanumeric and returns a true or false.
isAlpha()	Validates if the character passed is alpha and returns a true or false.

Programming Element:	Description:
isAscii()	Validates if the character passed is ascii and returns a true or false.
isWhiteSpace()	Validates if the character passed is white space and returns a true or false.
isControl()	Validates if the character passed is control character and returns a true or false.
isDigit()	Validates if the character passed is digit and returns a true or false.
isGraph()	Validates if the character passed is a printable character and returns a true or false.
isLowerCase()	Validates is the character passed is a lower case character and returns a true or false.
isPrintable()	Validates is the character passed is a printable character and returns a true or false.
isPunct()	Validates is the character passed is a punctuation character and returns a true or false.
isSpace()	Validates is the character passed is a space and returns a true or false.
isUpperCase()	Validates is the character passed is an uppercase character and returns a true or false.
randomSeed()	Used to initiate the random number generator. Pass an integer to generate the seed.
random()	Generates a random number between the specified range. Syntax is: random(minnum,maxnum);

Appendix 11
vi Editor Commands

At a command prompt (be it $ for normal user or # as super user) you need to type the following:

vi *filename*

Where filename is the name of the text file you need to edit. If the file does not exist, vi will create it when the editing work is saved.

After the vi editor is started, to enter "command mode" you need to press the [esc] key.

Exiting a vi Editing Session:

You must first press the [Esc] key to enter command mode before these keystrokes will work.

Keystrokes	Description
:q	Quit the editing session. If changes have been made and not saved, the editor will not exit.
:q!	Forces the ending of the editing session regardless of any changes made.
:w	Write (save) changes made to the file.
:wq	Write the changes to the file and then quit.
:wq!	Forces a write to the file and then quits

Inserting Text in the current file:

Keystroke	Description
i	Starts the insertion of text to the left of the cursor.
I	Starts inserting text at the beginning of the line that the cursor is on.
a	Starts appending text after the position of the cursor.
A	Starts appending text on the line that the cursor is on.
o	Causes text to be inserted on a new empty line below the position of the cursor.
O	Causes text to be inserted on a new empty line above the position of the cursor.
r	Replaces a single character at the location of the cursor.
R	Starts the replacement of characters (basically in overwrite mode) until the [Esc] key is pressed.

Deleting text in the current file:

Keystroke	Description
D	Delete from the cursor position to the end of the line.
dd	Delete the entire line the cursor is located on.
x	Delete the character to the right of the cursor.
X	Delete the character to the left of the cursor.

Copying text in the current file:

Keystroke	Description
y	Yank (copy) the text at the cursor.
yy	Copy the line at the cursor position.
p	Paste to the right of the cursor position.
P	Paste to the left of the cursor position.

Replacing & searching for text in the current file:

Keystroke	Description:
f	Search the current line for the character typed after the "f". If found, moves the cursor to that location.
/	Search downwards from the line the cursor is on for the text entered after the "/" command. If found, moves the cursor to that location.
?	Search upwards from the line the cursor is on for the text entered after the "/" command. If found, moves the cursor to that location.

Appendix 12

Common HTML Commands

Required:

1) 99% of Html commands are used as a pair.
2) All HTML documents will start with "<Html>" and end with "</Html>"
3) Most HTML documents have a "header" section that will begin with "<Head>" and end with "</Head>"
4) Below the header section, and required with all HTML documents is the "<Body>" command. Before the "</Html>" you will need to place a "</body>" command.
5) A skeletal HTML document therefore is:

<Html>
<Head>

</Head>
<Body>

</Body>
</Html>

6) Usually within the header section, a title tag (i.e., <Title> title goes here </Title>) is placed, but not required.

Html Tag	Description
<A> </A>	A hyper link anchor. Marks a hot spot. Within the "<A>" is the link information indicated by a href="xxxx" notation.
<b> </b>	Marks text between the two tags as bold.
<Body> </Body>	Marks the body of the Html document.
 	Does not need a closing </br>.

	Forces a page break.
<Center> </Center>	Used to center text on a page.
<Form> </Form>	Used to mark off an area in a page used as a form (i.e. user input section).
<H1> </H1>	Marks the text as a large header. H1 is largest.
<H2> </H2>	Marks the text as a large header. Smaller than H1. H1 through H6 is supported, with each being smaller than the previous.
<Head> </Head>	Marks the header section of the html document.
<html> </Html>	Marks beginning and end of Html.
<hr>	Does not need a closing </hr>. Used to draw a horizontal line on the screen.
<I> </I>	Marks text between the two tags as italic.
<Img>	Used to load an image. Does not need a closing </img>. Within the "<Img>" is the link information to the image indicated by a src="xx" notation.
<Input>	Does not need a closing </Input>. Used to denote an input field of a form. Needs to be within the section of a document marked by <Form> </Form> tags.
<Li> </Li>	A list entry. Used inside of a <UL> pair.
<P> </P>	Used to indicate a paragraph. The closing </P> causes an extra blank line to be shown.
<Title> </Title>	Indicates the document's title. Needs to be placed within the documents header.

<Table></Table>	Starts the creation of a table. Tables are a collection of row (<Tr>) and data (<Td>) within a row.
<Td> </Td>	A table data element. Used within a pair of <Tr>'s.
<Tr> </Tr>	A table row. Within a pair of <Tr>'s is sets of <Td>'s.
<U> </U>	Marks text between the two tags to be underlined.
<UL></UL>	For the creation of a list. Each list entry is marked by a pair of <Li> </Li>'s.

Appendix 13
Useful Tools and Other Sources

Make: Getting Started with Raspberry Pi: Getting to Know the Inexpensive ARM-power Linux Computer. By Matt Richardson & Shawn Wallace.

Make: Getting Started with Sensors: Measure the World with Electronics, Arduino, and Raspberry Pi. By Kimmo Karvinen & Tero Karvinen.

Make: Sensors. By Tero Karvinen, Kimmo Karvinen & Ville Valtokari.

Monk Makes: Electronic Starter Kit for Raspberry Pi.

Programming Arduino: Getting Started with Sketches. By Sion Monk.

Programming Arduino: Next Steps. Going Further with Sketches. By Simon Monk.

Programming the Raspberry Pi: Getting Started with Pythons. By Simon Monk.

Raspberry Pi Cookbook. By Simon Monk.

Raspberry PI for Dummies. By Sean McManus & Mike Cook

Raspberry Pi: puts fun back into computing!. By Mike McGrath.

Raspberry Pi: Quick Start Guide & Safety Instruction Manual. Element 14.

Raspberry Pi: User Guide. By Eben Upton & Gareth Halfacree.

References

Fritzing Component Library. www.Fritzing.org

http://arstechnica.com/information-technology/2015/02/raspberry-pi-2-
arrives-with-quad-core-cpu-1gb-ram-same-35-price/

http://blog.plurasight.com/linux-commands-for-beginners

http://downloads-element14.com/raspberrypi1.html

http://linksprite.com/wiki.index.php5?title=advanced_sensors_kit_for_Arduino

http://mvartan.com/2013/02/10/setting-up-a-headless-raspberry-pi/

http://openmicros.org/index.php/articles/94-ciseco-product-
documentation/raspberry-pi/217-getting-started-with-raspberry-pi-
gpio-and-python

http://ReadWrite.com/2014/06/27/Raspberry-pi-web-server-website-hosting

http://WeWorkWePlay.com/play/Automatically-Connect-a-Raspberry-Pi-to-a-
WiFi-Network/

http://WiringPi.com/pins/

http://wiringpi.com/wiringpi-and-the-raspberry-pi-compute-board/

http://www.chiark.GreenEnd.org/uk/~sgtatham/putty/download.html

http://www.CPlus.About.com/od/RaspberryPi/a/How-Do-I-Setup-SSH-On-
Raspberry-Pi.htm

http://www.dummies.com/how-to/content/linux-for-dummies-cheat-
sheet.html

http://www.fiz-ix.com/2013/02/direct-control-of-arduino-uno-digital-
inputoutput-pins-using-port-registers/

http://www.HowToGeek.com/139433/How-to-turn-a-raspberry-pi-into-a-
power-network-storage-device/

http://www.LinuxUser.co.uk/tutorials/build-a-file-server-with-the-raspberry-pi

http://www.MakeUseOf.com/Tag/Setting-Raspberry-Pi-Headless-SSH

http://www.PenguinTutor.com/Linux/RaspberryPi-Headless

http://www.pixelbeat.org/docs/linux_commands.html

http://www.RaspiPress.com/2013/05/turn-a-raspberry-pi-into-a-nas-network-
attached-storage-server/

https://Learn.AdaFruit.com/AdaFruits-Raspberry-Pi-Lesson-3-Network-
SetUp/Using-a-Wired-Network

https://Learn.AdaFruit.com/AdaFruits-Raspberry-Pi-Lesson-3-Network-
SetUp/Setting-Up-WiFi-With-Raspbain

https://tkkrlab.nl/wiki/arduino_37_sensors

https://www.arduino.cc/en/main/arduinoboarduno

https://www.JetBrains.com/Pycharm-edu/

https://www.Python.org/downloads/windows

https://www.sparkfun.com/products/retired/12994

Index

About the Author

Dr. Mike Stachiw is co-owner of Strategic Mapping and Data Services, LLC, a company dedicated to providing marketing support to all businesses, from the single entrepreneur to large corporations. Mike has over thirty years of experience in technology and its impact on business operations.

Since achieving the State Farmer Award while in the Future Farmers of America (FFA), he has been working in and around agriculture to better its future.

Mike's entry into the world of technology came when he built his first computer from a kit. Strategic Mapping and Data Services now provides extensive web hosting and database marketing services, including direct mail, and electronic newsletter distribution and fulfillment services to both large and small agribusiness firms.